KUMON MATH WORKBOOKS

Grade **4**

P9-DNI-176

Division

Table of Contents

KUMON

Addition & Subtraction Review

Date / /

Name

Score

/100

1 Calculate.

2 points per question

(1)
```
   2 5
 + 3 4
```

(2)
```
   3 8
 + 4 0
```

(3)
```
   3 2
 + 4 9
```

(4)
```
   5 7
 + 6 2
```

(5)
```
   7 6
 + 8 9
```

(6)
```
   5 3
 - 2 1
```

(7)
```
   4 6
 - 2 4
```

(8)
```
   3 2
 - 1 4
```

(9)
```
   6 0
 - 2 5
```

(10)
```
   5 4
 - 2 4
```

(11)
```
   6 4
 - 3 5
```

(12)
```
   5 3
 - 2 7
```

(13)
```
   7 5
 - 4 8
```

(14)
```
   6 2
 - 2 4
```

(15)
```
   9 6
 - 4 8
```

(16)
```
   5 4
 - 3 2
```

(17)
```
   3 5
 - 2 8
```

(18)
```
   8 2
 - 6 3
```

(19)
```
   5 0
 - 4 5
```

(20)
```
   6 4
 - 5 6
```

② Calculate.

3 points per question

(1)
```
  1 2 6
+   3 2
```

(2)
```
  1 4 7
+   2 8
```

(3)
```
  2 5 4
+ 1 3 5
```

(4)
```
  3 4 6
+ 2 3 7
```

(5)
```
  4 7 5
+ 3 4 8
```

(6)
```
  1 6 3
-   4 5
```

(7)
```
  2 8 5
-   6 7
```

(8)
```
  6 5 4
- 1 3 2
```

(9)
```
  4 7 3
- 1 2 5
```

(10)
```
  4 3 8
- 1 7 6
```

(11)
```
  5 3 2
- 2 8 0
```

(12)
```
  4 4 6
- 1 8 1
```

(13)
```
  7 5 3
- 2 0 9
```

(14)
```
  4 3 6
- 1 7 6
```

(15)
```
  7 6 8
- 5 1 9
```

(16)
```
  7 1 0
- 5 6 7
```

(17)
```
  8 0 2
- 2 3 4
```

(18)
```
  7 6 5
- 2 0 9
```

(19)
```
  4 0 5
- 2 4 3
```

(20)
```
  4 2 0
- 2 2 8
```

Do you remember your addition and subtraction?

2 Multiplication & Division Review

Level

Date / /

Name

Score

/100

1 Multiply.

2 points per question

(1)   2 4
    ×   2

(6)   5 4
    ×   7

(11)   2 4 7
     ×   6

(16)   3 2
     × 2 4

(2)   3 2
    ×   3

(7)   8 3
    ×   8

(12)   4 3 1
     ×   7

(17)   3 7
     × 4 5

(3)   1 8
    ×   4

(8)   1 2 6
    ×   2

(13)   3 4 5
     ×   8

(18)   5 3
     × 2 7

(4)   3 6
    ×   5

(9)   3 1 8
    ×   3

(14)   7 0 8
     ×   9

(19)   6 2
     × 5 4

(5)   2 7
    ×   6

(10)   4 2 3
     ×   4

(15)   2 3
     × 1 2

(20)   7 4
     × 6 3

2 Divide.

2 points per question

(1) $18 \div 2 =$

(2) $24 \div 3 =$

(3) $32 \div 4 =$

(4) $35 \div 5 =$

(5) $42 \div 6 =$

(6) $49 \div 7 =$

(7) $64 \div 8 =$

(8) $54 \div 9 =$

(9) $16 \div 2 =$

(10) $18 \div 3 =$

(11) $24 \div 4 =$

(12) $30 \div 6 =$

(13) $42 \div 7 =$

(14) $54 \div 8 =$

(15) $72 \div 9 =$

(16) $15 \div 2 =$

(17) $20 \div 3 =$

(18) $25 \div 4 =$

(19) $32 \div 5 =$

(20) $40 \div 6 =$

(21) $58 \div 7 =$

(22) $60 \div 8 =$

(23) $74 \div 9 =$

(24) $19 \div 2 =$

(25) $26 \div 3 =$

(26) $34 \div 4 =$

(27) $47 \div 5 =$

(28) $51 \div 7 =$

(29) $62 \div 8 =$

(30) $83 \div 9 =$

Do you remember your multiplication and division?

1 Subtract.

2 points per question

(1) 63
    −15

(2) 54
    −46

(3) 85
    −39

(4) 247
    −125

(5) 184
    − 92

(6) 700
    −423

(7) 520
    −246

(8) 403
    −237

(9) 314
    −162

(10) 852
     −348

2 Multiply.

2 points per question

(1) 46
    × 5

(2) 32
    × 2

(3) 54
    × 7

(4) 97
    × 6

(5) 27
    × 3

(6) 68
    × 9

(7) 387
    × 6

(8) 139
    × 5

(9) 480
    × 7

(10) 476
     × 4

(11) 608
     × 9

③ Multiply.

2 points per question

(1)
$$\begin{array}{r} 47 \\ \times\ 34 \\ \hline \end{array}$$

(3)
$$\begin{array}{r} 63 \\ \times\ 40 \\ \hline \end{array}$$

(5)
$$\begin{array}{r} 27 \\ \times\ 13 \\ \hline \end{array}$$

(7)
$$\begin{array}{r} 99 \\ \times\ 67 \\ \hline \end{array}$$

(2)
$$\begin{array}{r} 64 \\ \times\ 61 \\ \hline \end{array}$$

(4)
$$\begin{array}{r} 36 \\ \times\ 24 \\ \hline \end{array}$$

(6)
$$\begin{array}{r} 56 \\ \times\ 35 \\ \hline \end{array}$$

(8)
$$\begin{array}{r} 50 \\ \times\ 26 \\ \hline \end{array}$$

④ Divide.

3 points per question

(1) $29 \div 3 =$

(6) $16 \div 8 =$

(11) $33 \div 5 =$

(2) $45 \div 8 =$

(7) $32 \div 6 =$

(12) $80 \div 9 =$

(3) $63 \div 9 =$

(8) $44 \div 8 =$

(13) $65 \div 7 =$

(4) $52 \div 7 =$

(9) $27 \div 4 =$

(14) $78 \div 8 =$

(5) $43 \div 5 =$

(10) $56 \div 9 =$

How did you do? Let's check your work.

4 2-Digits ÷ 1-Digit

Date / /

Name

Level ★★

Score
/100

1 Divide.

5 points per question

(1)

$10 \div 2 = \boxed{}$ → vertical form → $\boxed{}$ ☜ Write the answer here.

$2\overline{)10}$

(2)

$14 \div 3 = \boxed{} R \boxed{}$ → vertical form → $\boxed{} R \boxed{}$ ☜ Write the remainder here.

$3\overline{)14}$

"R" means the "remainder."

2 Divide.

2 points per question

(1) $2\overline{)12}$

(2) $3\overline{)18}$

(3) $4\overline{)24}$

(4) $5\overline{)25}$

(5) $6\overline{)30}$

(6) $7\overline{)28}$

(7) $8\overline{)32}$

(8) $9\overline{)36}$

(9) $\boxed{}R\boxed{}$ $2\overline{)15}$

(10) $\boxed{}R\boxed{}$ $3\overline{)20}$

(11) $\boxed{}R\boxed{}$ $4\overline{)26}$

(12) $5\overline{)26}$

(13) $5\overline{)33}$

(14) $6\overline{)37}$

(15) $7\overline{)44}$

(16) $8\overline{)46}$

(17) $8\overline{)70}$

(18) $9\overline{)76}$

3 Divide.

2 points per question

(1) 2)26

(2) 2)28

(3) 2)40

(4) 2)42

(5) 2)44

(6) 2)46

(7) 2)48

(8) 2)60

(9) 2)64

(10) 2)80

(11) 2)30

(12) 2)32

(13) 2)36

(14) 2)52

(15) 3)36

(16) 3)39

(17) 3)60

(18) 3)63

(19) 3)69

(20) 3)42

(21) 3)48

(22) 3)54

(23) 3)57

(24) 3)72

(25) 3)81

(26) 3)87

(27) 3)99

Nice job! Let's keep going!

1 Divide.

2 points per question

(1) 3)24

(2) 3)33

(3) 3)48

(4) 3)51

(5) 3)69

(6) 3)75

(7) 4)44

(8) 4)48

(9) 4)52

(10) 4)64

(11) 4)76

(12) 4)80

(13) 4)72

(14) 4)60

(15) 4)68

(16) 4)56

(17) 4)84

(18) 4)96

(19) 4)32

(20) 4)24

(21) 4)36

(22) 4)28

(23) 4)40

(24) 4)88

(25) 4)92

© Kumon Publishing Co., Ltd.

2 **Divide.**

(1) 5)15

(2) 5)25

(3) 5)40

(4) 5)75

(5) 5)55

(6) 5)65

(7) 5)80

(8) 5)90

(9) 5)85

(10) 5)95

(11) 6)24

(12) 6)30

(13) 6)48

(14) 6)54

(15) 6)66

(16) 6)72

(17) 6)84

(18) 6)78

(19) 6)96

(20) 6)90

(21) 3)51

(22) 2)52

(23) 4)52

(24) 3)54

(25) 2)54

Nice work! Now let's check your score!

6 2-Digits ÷ 1-Digit

Date / / Name

Level ★★

Score /100

1 Divide.

2 points per question

(1) 2)56

(2) 4)56

(3) 7)56

(4) 8)56

(5) 2)60

(6) 3)60

(7) 4)60

(8) 5)60

(9) 6)60

(10) 3)63

(11) 7)63

(12) 9)63

(13) 2)66

(14) 3)66

(15) 6)66

(16) 2)70

(17) 5)70

(18) 7)70

(19) 2)72

(20) 3)72

(21) 4)72

(22) 6)72

(23) 8)72

(24) 9)72

(25) 7)77

12 © Kumon Publishing Co., Ltd.

2 Divide.

2 points per question

(1)
$$2\overline{)78}$$

(2)
$$3\overline{)78}$$

(3)
$$6\overline{)78}$$

(4)
$$2\overline{)80}$$

(5)
$$4\overline{)80}$$

(6)
$$5\overline{)80}$$

(7)
$$8\overline{)80}$$

(8)
$$3\overline{)81}$$

(9)
$$9\overline{)81}$$

(10)
$$3\overline{)84}$$

(11)
$$4\overline{)84}$$

(12)
$$6\overline{)84}$$

(13)
$$7\overline{)84}$$

(14)
$$2\overline{)90}$$

(15)
$$3\overline{)90}$$

(16)
$$5\overline{)90}$$

(17)
$$6\overline{)90}$$

(18)
$$9\overline{)90}$$

(19)
$$2\overline{)96}$$

(20)
$$3\overline{)96}$$

(21)
$$4\overline{)96}$$

(22)
$$6\overline{)96}$$

(23)
$$8\overline{)96}$$

(24)
$$3\overline{)99}$$

(25)
$$9\overline{)99}$$

Are you getting the hang of it?
Let's keep going!

2-Digits ÷ 1-Digit

Date / /

Name

1 Divide.

2 points per question

(1) 2)1 3 □R□

(2) 2)2 5 □□R□

(3) 2)3 1

(4) 2)4 3

(5) 2)5 7

(6) 2)6 1

(7) 3)2 6

(8) 3)3 7

(9) 3)4 4

(10) 3)5 3 □□R□

(11) 3)5 5

(12) 3)6 1

(13) 3)6 5

(14) 4)3 2

(15) 4)3 8

(16) 4)4 7

(17) 4)5 3

(18) 4)6 0

(19) 4)6 1

(20) 4)6 5

(21) 5)5 2

(22) 5)5 8

(23) 5)6 0

(24) 5)6 1

(25) 5)6 9

14 © Kumon Publishing Co., Ltd.

② Divide.

2 points per question

(1) 2)37

(2) 2)41

(3) 2)55

(4) 2)63

(5) 3)34

(6) 3)47

(7) 3)58

(8) 3)62

(9) 4)49

(10) 4)59

(11) 4)60

(12) 4)66

(13) 5)67

(14) 5)69

(15) 5)71

(16) 5)73

(17) 5)74

(18) 6)74

(19) 7)74

(20) 8)74

(21) 9)74

(22) 6)75

(23) 7)75

(24) 8)75

(25) 9)75

Don't forget to check your answers when you're done.

15

8

2-Digits ÷ 1-Digit

Date / /

Name

Level ★★

Score

/100

1 **Divide.**

2 points per question

(1) 2)76

(2) 4)76

(3) 5)76

(4) 6)76

(5) 7)76

(6) 8)76

(7) 9)76

(8) 2)77

(9) 3)77

(10) 5)77

(11) 6)77

(12) 7)77

(13) 8)77

(14) 9)77

(15) 2)78

(16) 3)78

(17) 4)78

(18) 6)78

(19) 7)78

(20) 8)78

(21) 9)78

(22) 2)79

(23) 3)79

(24) 4)79

(25) 5)79

© Kumon Publishing Co., Ltd.

2 Divide.

2 points per question

(1) 6)79

(2) 7)79

(3) 8)79

(4) 9)79

(5) 2)80

(6) 3)80

(7) 4)80

(8) 5)80

(9) 7)80

(10) 8)80

(11) 9)80

(12) 2)82

(13) 3)82

(14) 4)82

(15) 5)82

(16) 6)82

(17) 8)82

(18) 9)82

(19) 2)83

(20) 3)83

(21) 4)83

(22) 5)83

(23) 6)83

(24) 7)83

(25) 9)83

If you made a mistake, just try the problem again.
You can do it!

1   Divide.

2 points per question

(1)   2)85

(2)   4)85

(3)   5)85

(4)   6)85

(5)   7)85

(6)   8)85

(7)   9)85

(8)   2)87

(9)   3)87

(10)   5)87

(11)   6)87

(12)   7)87

(13)   8)87

(14)   9)87

(15)   2)89

(16)   3)89

(17)   4)89

(18)   6)89

(19)   7)89

(20)   8)89

(21)   9)89

(22)   2)90

(23)   3)90

(24)   4)90

(25)   5)90

2 Divide.

2 points per question

(1) 6)90

(2) 7)90

(3) 8)90

(4) 9)90

(5) 2)91

(6) 3)91

(7) 4)91

(8) 5)91

(9) 7)91

(10) 8)91

(11) 9)91

(12) 2)93

(13) 3)93

(14) 4)93

(15) 5)93

(16) 6)93

(17) 8)93

(18) 9)93

(19) 3)94

(20) 4)94

(21) 5)94

(22) 6)94

(23) 7)94

(24) 8)94

(25) 9)94

Now let's try something a bit different!

10

3-Digits ÷ 1-Digit

Level
★★

Score

/100

Date   /   /

Name

1 **Divide.**

2 points per question

(1)   2)246

(2)   2)240

(3)   2)624

(4)   2)846

(5)   2)840

(6)   3)369

(7)   3)639

(8)   3)960

(9)   4)448

(10) 4)840

(11) 2)228

(12) 2)230

(13) 2)232

(14) 2)458

(15) 2)636

(16) 3)345

(17) 3)657

(18) 3)675

(19) 4)456

(20) 4)472

2 Divide.

(1)
$$2 \overline{)\ 1\ 2\ 0}$$

(2)
$$3 \overline{)\ 1\ 2\ 0}$$

(3)
$$4 \overline{)\ 1\ 2\ 0}$$

(4)
$$5 \overline{)\ 1\ 2\ 0}$$

(5)
$$6 \overline{)\ 1\ 2\ 0}$$

(6)
$$8 \overline{)\ 1\ 2\ 0}$$

(7)
$$9 \overline{)\ 1\ 2\ 6}$$

(8)
$$2 \overline{)\ 1\ 2\ 8}$$

(9)
$$3 \overline{)\ 1\ 2\ 6}$$

(10)
$$4 \overline{)\ 1\ 2\ 8}$$

(11)
$$5 \overline{)\ 1\ 3\ 0}$$

(12)
$$7 \overline{)\ 1\ 4\ 0}$$

(13)
$$8 \overline{)\ 1\ 4\ 4}$$

(14)
$$9 \overline{)\ 1\ 4\ 4}$$

(15)
$$3 \overline{)\ 1\ 5\ 6}$$

(16)
$$4 \overline{)\ 1\ 5\ 6}$$

(17)
$$6 \overline{)\ 1\ 6\ 8}$$

(18)
$$7 \overline{)\ 1\ 6\ 8}$$

(19)
$$8 \overline{)\ 1\ 6\ 8}$$

(20)
$$9 \overline{)\ 1\ 7\ 1}$$

That's good. Let's practice some more!

1 Divide.

2 points per question

(1)
2) 2 2 4

(2)
4) 2 2 8

(3)
6) 2 3 4

(4)
7) 2 3 8

(5)
8) 2 5 6

(6)
9) 2 6 1

(7)
3) 3 4 8

(8)
5) 3 4 5

(9)
7) 3 6 4

(10)
8) 3 6 8

(11)
9) 3 7 8

(12)
2) 4 3 6

(13)
4) 4 6 0

(14)
6) 4 6 2

(15)
7) 4 6 2

(16)
8) 4 6 4

(17)
9) 4 6 8

(18)
2) 5 1 2

(19)
3) 5 1 3

(20)
4) 5 2 4

2 Divide.

(1) 7)616

(2) 8)608

(3) 9)612

(4) 2)630

(5) 4)660

(6) 5)630

(7) 7)630

(8) 9)630

(9) 3)300

(10) 3)306

(11) 3)318 → 1 0 □

(12) 3)618 → □ 0 □

(13) 3)624

(14) 4)412

(15) 2)618

(16) 4)812

(17) 5)515

(18) 6)618

(19) 7)721

(20) 8)816

Don't forget to check your work when you're done.

3-Digits ÷ 1-Digit

Level

★★

Score

/ 100

Date
/ /

Name

1 Divide.

2 points per question

(1) 2)612

(2) 4)756

(3) 6)612

(4) 7)756

(5) 8)752

(6) 9)756

(7) 3)816

(8) 5)820

(9) 7)819

(10) 8)824

(11) 9)810

(12) 2)140

(13) 4)428

(14) 6)636

(15) 7)686

(16) 8)720

(17) 9)729

(18) 2)818

(19) 3)903

(20) 5)945

2 Divide.

3 points per question

(1) 6)852

(2) 7)763

(3) 9)945

(4) 2)416

(5) 3)321

(6) 4)576

(7) 7)742

(8) 8)832

(9) 3)438

(10) 4)636

(11) 5)525

(12) 6)330

(13) 8)416

(14) 9)234

(15) 4)392

(16) 5)380

(17) 6)240

(18) 7)735

(19) 8)848

(20) 9)963

Practice makes perfect. Let's keep going!

Level ★★

Date / /

Name

Score /100

1 **Divide.**

2 points per question

(1) 2)616

(2) 4)636

(3) 6)642

(4) 7)644

(5) 8)672

(6) 9)675

(7) 3)678

(8) 5)680

(9) 6)684

(10) 8)688

(11) 9)693

(12) 2)696

(13) 4)696

(14) 6)702

(15) 7)714

(16) 8)712

(17) 9)720

(18) 2)720

(19) 3)720

(20) 5)720

2 Divide.

(1)
6⟌720

(2)
7⟌728

(3)
9⟌738

(4)
2⟌748

(5)
3⟌750

(6)
4⟌752

(7)
5⟌760

(8)
8⟌768

(9)
9⟌774

(10)
3⟌786

(11)
4⟌788

(12)
5⟌790

(13)
6⟌792

(14)
8⟌800

(15)
9⟌801

(16)
3⟌804

(17)
4⟌812

(18)
7⟌812

(19)
8⟌816

(20)
9⟌819

You're doing really well!

14 3-Digits ÷ 1-Digit

1 Divide.

2 points per question

(1) 2)820

(2) 4)824

(3) 6)828

(4) 7)833

(5) 8)840

(6) 2)846

(7) 3)846

(8) 5)850

(9) 6)852

(10) 7)854

(11) 9)864

(12) 3)864

(13) 6)870

(14) 7)875

(15) 8)872

(16) 9)873

(17) 2)874

(18) 3)876

(19) 4)876

(20) 5)880

2 Divide.

3 points per question

(1) 2)871 □□□ R □

(2) 2)457

(3) 3)458

(4) 4)634

(5) 5)333

(6) 6)333

(7) 7)333

(8) 8)333

(9) 3)401

(10) 4)401

(11) 6)401

(12) 7)401

(13) 8)401

(14) 9)401

(15) 2)517

(16) 3)517

(17) 5)517

(18) 6)517

(19) 7)517

(20) 9)517

You've made a lot of progress.
Keep up the good work!

3-Digits ÷ 1-Digit

Date / /

Name

Level ★★

Score /100

1 Divide.

2 points per question

(1) 2)576

(2) 4)576

(3) 6)576

(4) 7)576

(5) 8)576

(6) 9)576

(7) 3)601

(8) 5)601

(9) 7)601

(10) 8)601

(11) 9)601

(12) 2)777

(13) 4)777

(14) 6)777

(15) 7)777

(16) 8)777

(17) 9)777

(18) 2)801

(19) 3)801

(20) 5)801

② Divide.

(1) 7)801

(2) 8)801

(3) 9)801

(4) 3)853

(5) 5)853

(6) 7)853

(7) 8)853

(8) 9)853

(9) 2)441

(10) 3)628

(11) 4)581

(12) 6)613

(13) 8)468

(14) 9)367

(15) 3)320

(16) 4)422

(17) 5)519

(18) 6)256

(19) 7)732

(20) 9)260

Great work! Let's move on to some bigger numbers!

31

4-Digits ÷ 1-Digit

Date / /

Name

Score

/100

1 Divide.

4 points per question

(1) ☐☐☐
2)1246

(2) 5)1205

(3) 6)1200

(4) 7)1673

(5) 9)2052

(6) 3)2529

(7) 6)2562

(8) 4)3632

(9) 7)3633

(10) ☐☐☐☐
2)4160

(11) 4)4076

(12) 8)4144

② Divide.

(1)

$$2 \overline{) 5030}$$

(2)

$$4 \overline{) 5036}$$

(3)

$$6 \overline{) 5034}$$

(4)

$$3 \overline{) 7032}$$

(5)

$$5 \overline{) 7035}$$

(6)

$$7 \overline{) 7035}$$

(7)

$$9 \overline{) 8001}$$

(8)

$$2 \overline{) 8012}$$

(9)

$$6 \overline{) 8004}$$

(10)

$$7 \overline{) 8001}$$

(11)

$$3 \overline{) 9006}$$

(12)

$$4 \overline{) 9068}$$

(13)

$$9 \overline{) 9603}$$

Don't forget to check your answers when you're done!

4-Digits ÷ 1-Digit

Date / /

Name

Level

Score  /100

1 Divide.

4 points per question

(1) 8)5224

(2) 6)4608

(3) ☐☐☐R☐ 4)2686

(4) 2)1091

(5) 7)3602

(6) 3)1747

(7) 4)5817

(8) 6)6133

(9) 8)5000

(10) 9)3679

(11) 3)3103

(12) 5)5193

34   © Kumon Publishing Co., Ltd.

② Divide.

(1) 8)2872

(2) 6)1218

(3) 4)3640

(4) 9)6138

(5) 7)3276

(6) 5)2340

(7) 8)7576

(8) 4)6132

(9) 3)6078

(10) 8)6935

(11) 7)5989

(12) 4)3458

(13) 3)3926

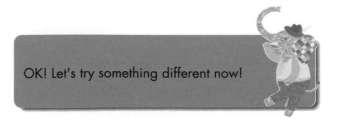

OK! Let's try something different now!

Level ★★

Date   /   /

Name

Score   /100

1   Divide.

5 points per question

(1)

```
         2  R 3  ← remainder
21)  4  5
     4  2  ← 21×2
        3  ← 45−42
```

(5)

```
       □ R □
21)  6  5
     □□
      □
```

(9)

```
       □ R □□
21)  7  8
     □□
     □□
```

(2)

```
         2  R □
21)  4  7
     □□  ← 21×2
      □
```

(6)

```
21)  6  9
```

(10)

```
21)  8  5
```

(3)

```
       □ R □
21)  4  8
     □□
      □
```

(7)

```
         3  R □
21)  7  0
     □□
      □
```

(4)

```
21)  4  9
```

(8)

```
21)  7  2
```

2 Divide.

(1)
```
        □ R □
21 ) 8 6
    □ □
      □
```

(2)
```
21 ) 8 7
```

(3)
```
21 ) 8 9
```

(4)
```
21 ) 9 4
```

(5)
```
21 ) 9 9
```

(6)
```
          □ R □
21 ) 1 0 7
    □ □ □
        □
```

(7)
```
21 ) 1 0 9
```

(8)
```
21 ) 1 2 7
```

(9)
```
21 ) 1 2 9
```

(10)
```
21 ) 1 1 9
```

If you're not sure about your answer, it never hurts to try again!

37

3-Digits ÷ 2-Digits

Score

/100

Date / /

Name

1 Divide.

5 points per question

(1)
21)88

(2)
21)84

(3)
21)83

(4)
21)90

(5)
21)82

(6)
21)95

(7)
21)108

(8)
21)105

(9)
21)102

(10)
21)110

2 Divide.

5 points per question

(1) 21)130

(2) 21)135

(3) 21)148

(4) 21)147

(5) 21)145

(6) 21)168

(7) 21)165

(8) 21)178

(9) 21)189

(10) 21)204

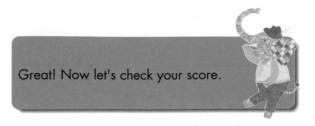

Great! Now let's check your score.

3-Digits ÷ 2-Digits

Date   /   /

Name

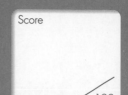

Score

/100

1 Divide.

5 points per question

(1) 31)65

(2) 31)75

(3) 31)99

(4) 31)90

(5) 31)95

(6) 31)110

(7) 31)125

(8) 31)120

(9) 31)130

(10) 31)140

2 Divide.

5 points per question

(1) 31)145

(2) 31)155

(3) 31)150

(4) 31)185

(5) 31)190

(6) 31)215

(7) 31)220

(8) 31)245

(9) 31)250

(10) 31)300

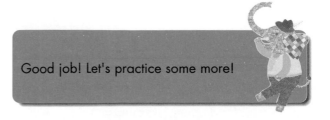

Good job! Let's practice some more!

1 **Divide.**

5 points per question

(1)

41)85

(2)

41)81

(3)

41)125

(4)

41)123

(5)

41)121

(6)

41)165

(7)

41)163

(8)

41)208

(9)

41)205

(10)

41)235

2 Divide.

(1) 41) 2 4 8

(2) 41) 2 4 6

(3) 41) 2 4 4

(4) 41) 2 8 0

(5) 41) 2 9 0

(6) 41) 3 2 0

(7) 41) 3 3 0

(8) 41) 3 6 0

(9) 41) 3 7 0

(10) 41) 4 0 0

Remember, just take it step by step!
You're doing really well!

3-Digits ÷ 2-Digits

Date   /   /

Name

Level

Score

/100

1 Divide.

4 points per question

(1) 22)66

(2) 22)75

(3) 22)88

(4) 22)100

(5) 22)110

(6) 22)125

(7) 22)132

(8) 22)145

(9) 22)154

(10) 22)165

(11) 22)185

(12) 22)200

2 Divide.

(1) $23\overline{)46}$

(2) $23\overline{)70}$

(3) $23\overline{)95}$

(4) $23\overline{)120}$

(5) $23\overline{)145}$

(6) $23\overline{)170}$

(7) $23\overline{)200}$

(8) $32\overline{)70}$

(9) $32\overline{)110}$

(10) $32\overline{)160}$

(11) $32\overline{)200}$

(12) $32\overline{)250}$

(13) $32\overline{)300}$

Don't forget to check your answers when you're done!

3-Digits ÷ 2-Digits

1 **Divide.**

4 points per question

(1) 33)99

(5) 33)255

(9) 42)180

(2) □R□ 33)135 □□□ □

(6) 33)300

(10) 42)210

(3) 33)165

(7) 42)120

(11) 42)300

(4) 33)215

(8) 42)150

(12) 42)400

2 Divide.

(1) 43)100

(2) 43)150

(3) 43)215

(4) 43)280

(5) 43)340

(6) 43)400

(7) 24)80

(8) 24)96

(9) 24)110

(10) 24)120

(11) 24)150

(12) 24)185

(13) 24)220

If a problem looks tricky, just think about it a bit more.

47

3-Digits ÷ 2-Digits

Level ★★

Score /100

1 Divide.

4 points per question

(1) 34)90

(2) 34)130

(3) 34)170

(4) 34)210

(5) 34)255

(6) 34)310

(7) 25)110

(8) 25)125

(9) 25)175

(10) 25)210

(11) 25)225

(12) 25)240

2 Divide.

4 points per question

(1)
$$27 \overline{)110}$$

(2)
$$27 \overline{)135}$$

(3)
$$27 \overline{)162}$$

(4)
$$27 \overline{)190}$$

(5)
$$27 \overline{)216}$$

(6)
$$27 \overline{)250}$$

(7)
$$36 \overline{)100}$$

(8)
$$36 \overline{)144}$$

(9)
$$36 \overline{)160}$$

(10)
$$36 \overline{)180}$$

(11)
$$36 \overline{)215}$$

(12)
$$36 \overline{)252}$$

(13)
$$36 \overline{)340}$$

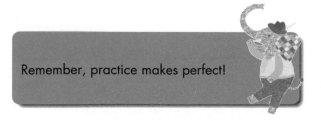

Remember, practice makes perfect!

3-Digits ÷ 2-Digits

1 **Divide.**

4 points per question

(1) 37)115

(2) 37)150

(3) 37)185

(4) 37)230

(5) 37)259

(6) 37)300

(7) 44)132

(8) 44)180

(9) 44)220

(10) 44)280

(11) 44)352

(12) 44)400

2 Divide.

(1) 45)180

(2) 45)230

(3) 45)270

(4) 45)310

(5) 45)360

(6) 45)420

(7) 47)150

(8) 47)200

(9) 47)235

(10) 47)282

(11) 47)330

(12) 47)376

(13) 47)430

Great! Now let's check your score.

26 3-Digits ÷ 2-Digits

Date / /

Name

Level ★★

Score

/100

1 Divide.

4 points per question

(1)

54)110

(2)

54)150

(3)

54)220

(4)

55)350

(5)

55)440

(6)

55)500

(7)

63)130

(8)

63)200

(9)

63)260

(10)

64)360

(11)

64)480

(12)

64)600

2 Divide.

4 points per question

(1) 56)110

(2) 56)190

(3) 56)280

(4) 57)350

(5) 57)450

(6) 57)550

(7) 65)140

(8) 65)200

(9) 65)260

(10) 66)300

(11) 66)360

(12) 66)480

(13) 66)600

Keep up the great work!

1 **Divide.**

4 points per question

(1)
$$61\overline{)186}$$

(2)
$$62\overline{)186}$$

(3)
$$62\overline{)305}$$

(4)
$$63\overline{)305}$$

(5)
$$63\overline{)441}$$

(6)
$$64\overline{)441}$$

(7)
$$71\overline{)216}$$

(8)
$$72\overline{)216}$$

(9)
$$72\overline{)355}$$

(10)
$$73\overline{)355}$$

(11)
$$73\overline{)511}$$

(12)
$$74\overline{)511}$$

2 Divide.

(1) 81) 2 5 2

(2) 82) 2 5 2

(3) 82) 4 1 5

(4) 83) 4 1 5

(5) 83) 7 5 6

(6) 84) 7 5 6

(7) 91) 2 7 6

(8) 92) 2 7 6

(9) 92) 4 6 5

(10) 93) 4 6 5

(11) 93) 6 4 4

(12) 94) 6 4 4

(13) 94) 8 4 6

Don't forget to show your parents how far you've come!

3-Digits ÷ 2-Digits

Date
/   /

Name

 Level ★★

 Score
/100

1 Divide.

4 points per question

(1) 75)152

(2) 75)225

(3) 75)375

(4) 75)456

(5) 75)560

(6) 75)675

(7) 76)304

(8) 76)456

(9) 76)500

(10) 76)525

(11) 76)608

(12) 76)675

2 Divide.

4 points per question

(1)

$85 \overline{)255}$

(2)

$85 \overline{)344}$

(3)

$85 \overline{)425}$

(4)

$85 \overline{)516}$

(5)

$86 \overline{)425}$

(6)

$86 \overline{)688}$

(7)

$86 \overline{)765}$

(8)

$95 \overline{)384}$

(9)

$95 \overline{)475}$

(10)

$95 \overline{)700}$

(11)

$96 \overline{)475}$

(12)

$96 \overline{)700}$

(13)

$96 \overline{)864}$

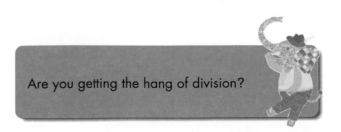

Are you getting the hang of division?

3-Digits ÷ 2-Digits

Date / /

Name

Level
★ ★

Score

/100

1 Divide.

4 points per question

(1) 29)90

(2) 29)116

(3) 29)120

(4) 29)140

(5) 29)154

(6) 29)168

(7) 29)180

(8) 29)203

(9) 29)220

(10) 29)252

(11) 29)262

(12) 29)271

2 Divide.

(1) 39)81

(2) 39)117

(3) 39)193

(4) 39)236

(5) 39)273

(6) 39)346

(7) 39)368

(8) 49)100

(9) 49)147

(10) 49)192

(11) 49)263

(12) 49)384

(13) 49)465

Don't forget to check your answers when you're done!

1 **Divide.**

4 points per question

(1) 59)120

(2) 59)177

(3) 59)232

(4) 59)360

(5) 59)464

(6) 59)550

(7) 69)150

(8) 69)215

(9) 69)352

(10) 69)410

(11) 69)500

(12) 69)656

② Divide.

4 points per question

(1)

79)240

(2)

79)322

(3)

79)514

(4)

79)630

(5)

79)720

(6)

89)270

(7)

89)462

(8)

89)545

(9)

89)620

(10)

89)840

(11)

99)290

(12)

99)470

(13)

99)950

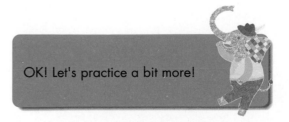

OK! Let's practice a bit more!

3-Digits ÷ 2-Digits

Date / /

Name

Level ☆☆

Score

/100

1 Divide.

4 points per question

(1) 48) 1 4 7

(2) 49) 1 4 7

(3) 49) 3 4 8

(4) 58) 3 4 8

(5) 58) 5 5 0

(6) 59) 5 5 0

(7) 13) 9 1

(8) 14) 9 1

(9) 15) 1 2 0

(10) 16) 1 2 0

(11) 18) 1 4 4

(12) 19) 1 4 4

2 Divide.

(1)
28)154

(2)
28)271

(3)
29)120

(4)
29)182

(5)
29)257

(6)
64)310

(7)
65)407

(8)
66)453

(9)
74)592

(10)
75)660

(11)
85)595

(12)
86)780

(13)
96)665

Excellent! Now let's look at division a different way.

32

Checking the Answer

Level ☆☆

Date　　/　　/

Name

Score
　　　/100

1 Write the appropriate number in each box.

5 points per question

(1) $31 \div 4 = \boxed{} \text{ R } \boxed{}$

(2) $31 = 4 \times \boxed{} + \boxed{}$
　　　└ Write the largest number possible in this box.

(3) $46 \div 7 = \boxed{} \text{ R } \boxed{}$

(4) $46 = 7 \times \boxed{} + \boxed{}$
　　　└ Write the largest number possible in this box.

(5) $68 \div 12 = \boxed{} \text{ R } \boxed{}$

(6) $68 = 12 \times \boxed{} + \boxed{}$
　　　└ Write the largest number possible in this box.

2 Divide and then recalculate the problem. This is also known as checking your answer.

10 points per question

(1)

$$6 \text{ R } \boxed{}$$
$$28\overline{)191}$$
$$\boxed{}$$
$$\overline{\boxed{}}$$

$191 \div 28 = \boxed{} \text{ R } \boxed{}$

$191 = 28 \times \boxed{} + \boxed{}$

⟨Recalculate⟩
$$\begin{array}{r} 2\,8 \\ \times \quad 6 \\ \hline \boxed{} \\ \downarrow\downarrow\downarrow \\ \boxed{} \\ +\ \boxed{} \\ \hline 1\,9\,1 \end{array}$$

(2)

$$43\overline{)227}$$

$227 \div 43 = \boxed{} \text{ R } \boxed{}$

$227 = 43 \times \boxed{} + \boxed{}$

⟨Recalculate⟩
$$\begin{array}{r} 4\,3 \\ \times \quad \boxed{} \\ \hline \boxed{} \\ \downarrow\downarrow\downarrow \\ \boxed{} \\ +\ \boxed{} \\ \hline \boxed{} \end{array}$$

3 Divide and then recalculate the problem.

10 points per question

(1)

$53 \overline{) 3\ 8\ 6}$

$386 = 53 \times \square + \square\square$

⟨Recalculate⟩

$$\begin{array}{r} 5\ 3 \\ \times\ \ \square \\ \hline \end{array}$$

(2)

$64 \overline{) 4\ 2\ 8}$

$428 = 64 \times \square + \square\square$

⟨Recalculate⟩

(3)

$76 \overline{) 5\ 3\ 0}$

$530 =$

⟨Recalculate⟩

(4)

$89 \overline{) 7\ 0\ 0}$

$700 =$

⟨Recalculate⟩

(5)

$99 \overline{) 7\ 8\ 2}$

$782 =$

⟨Recalculate⟩

Did you find any mistakes when you recalculated to check your answers?

3-Digits ÷ 2-Digits

33

Date   /   /

Name

Level
★★

Score

/100

---

1 **Divide.**

5 points per question

(1)
```
          1 □ R □
    21)2 7 7
      2 1
        6 7
        □□
         □
```

(2)
```
          4 □ R □
    21)8 8 7
      □□
      □□
      □□
       □
```

(3)
```
        □□ R □
    21)9 4 7
      □□
      □□□
      □□□
        □
```

(4)
```
    21)4 8 6
```

(5)
```
        □□ R □□
    21)6 8 3
      □□
      □□
      □□
      □□
```

(6)
```
    21)9 6 5
```

(7)
```
    31)9 6 5
```

(8)
```
    31)6 5 4
```

(9)
```
    31)4 3 6
```

2 Divide.

5 points per question

(1) 41)865

(5)
```
        3 □ R □
21)6 3 5
   □ □
      □
```

(9) 31)945

(2) 41)908

(6) 21)645

(10) 31)960

(3) 41)496

(7) 21)843

(11) 31)623

(4) 41)957

(8) 21)854

Great! Now let's check your answers.

34 3-Digits ÷ 2-Digits

Date / /

Name

Level ★★

Score

／100

1 Divide.

5 points per question

(1)

　　□□R□□
21)2 8 5

(5)

26)2 8 1

(9)

31)9 7 4

(2)

22)4 8 8

(6)

27)3 1 0

(10)

32)6 0 0

(3)

23)7 0 3

(7)

28)5 7 4

(11)

33)9 7 4

(4)

24)9 7 2

(8)

29)9 5 9

(12)

34)7 1 5

② Divide.

4 points per question

(1) 37)762

(2) 38)974

(3) 39)800

(4) 40)915

(5) 44)974

(6) 46)974

(7) 48)974

(8) 53)817

(9) 55)817

(10) 57)817

Nice job! Let's keep going!

35

3-Digits ÷ 2-Digits

Level

Date
/ /

Name

Score
/100

1 Divide.

5 points per question

(1)

29)885

(5)

31)885

(9)

25)885

(2)

39)946

(6)

41)946

(10)

35)946

(3)

49)987

(7)

51)987

(11)

45)987

(4)

59)770

(8)

61)770

(12)

55)770

② Divide.

4 points per question

(1)

25)794

(5)

31)956

(9)

43)932

(2)

36)730

(6)

52)989

(10)

56)824

(3)

21)885

(7)

28)989

(4)

42)642

(8)

37)863

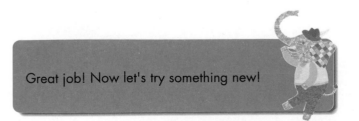

Great job! Now let's try something new!

1 **Divide.**

5 points per question

(1)
```
        6 □ R □
   21) 1 3 4 5
      □□□
       □□
       □□
        □
```

(4)
```
   21) 1 0 9 7
```

(7)
```
   31) 1 2 8 5
```

(2)
```
      □□ R □
   21) 1 4 5 6
```

(5)
```
   21) 1 3 0 0
```

(8)
```
   31) 1 6 7 8
```

(3)
```
      □□ R □□
   21) 1 5 6 7
```

(6)
```
   21) 1 9 9 0
```

(9)
```
   31) 2 6 0 0
```

2 Divide.

5 points per question

(1) 41)1345

(5)
```
        4 □ R □
31) 1 2 4 5
    □ □ □
        □
```

(9)
```
      □ □ R □
25) 1 0 0 4
```

(2) 41)2123

(6) 31)1255

(10) 28)1125

(3) 41)2987

(7) 31)1575

(11) 35)1754

(4) 41)4000

(8) 31)1880

Let's try some even bigger numbers now!

4-Digits ÷ 2-Digits

Date / /

Name

Score

/100

1 Divide.

5 points per question

(1) 35)1435

(2) 37)1435

(3) 39)1435

(4) 41)1435

(5) 42)2345

(6) 44)2345

(7) 48)2345

(8) 50)2345

(9) 51)3456

(10) 53)3456

(11) 57)3456

(12) 65)3456

2 Divide.

4 points per question

(1) 55)4000

(2) 56)4000

(3) 58)4000

(4) 60)4000

(5) 39)2357

(6) 41)2357

(7) 43)3981

(8) 51)3981

(9) 54)4857

(10) 68)4857

Great work! Now let's check your score!

1 Divide.

6 points per question

(1)
```
         □ □ □ R □
   21) 4 8 7 6
       4 2
         6 7
         6 3
         □ □
         □ □
           □
```

(4)
```
   31) 8 9 0 2
```

(2)
```
   21) 6 7 8 9
```

(5)
```
   31) 6 7 9 9
```

(3)
```
         □ □ □ R □
   21) 5 6 7 8
       □ □
       □ □ □
       □ □ □
           □
```

(6)
```
         □ □ □ R □ □
   32) 6 4 2 1
       □ □
       □ □
         □ □
```

② Divide.

8 points per question

(1)

32⟌6890

(2)

32⟌4000

(3)

41⟌6789

(4)

42⟌6789

(5)

42⟌8412

(6)

43⟌8412

(7)

43⟌8902

(8)

44⟌8902

Now we can move on to division with even larger numbers!

Division of Large Numbers

39

Level ★★★

Date / /

Name

Score /100

1 Divide.

6 points per question

(1)
```
       □ R □
123) 5 0 1
     □ □ □
         □
```

(2)
```
       □ R □ □
164) 9 9 7
```

(3)
```
237) 9 4 8
```

(4)
```
273) 9 6 5
```

(5)
```
306) 9 5 7
```

(6)
```
342) 8 1 9
```

2 Divide.

8 points per question

(1)

```
        □ □ R □ □
213) 8 9 7 6
     □ □ □
       □ □ □
       □ □ □
         □ □
```

(2)

223) 8 9 7 6

(3)

243) 8 9 7 6

(4)

253) 8 9 7 6

(5)

263) 8 9 7 6

(6)

273) 8 9 7 6

(7)

283) 8 9 7 6

(8)

293) 8 9 7 6

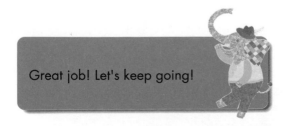

Great job! Let's keep going!

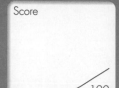
1 **Divide.**

6 points per question

(1)

71)946

(4)

74)946

(2)

71)4357

(5)

74)4357

(3)

713)9872

(6)

746)9087

© Kumon Publishing Co., Ltd.

2 Divide.

(1) 82)946

(2) 82)4357

(3) 824)9891

(4) 835)98721

(5) 90)946

(6) 90)4357

(7) 902)9891

(8) 913)98721

Now let's mix it up. You can do it!

Mixed Calculations

Date / /

Name

Level ★★★

Score /100

1 Calculate the expression in parentheses first, and then solve the problem.

2 points per question

(1) $9-(5-2)=9-\square$
$=$

(2) $9-(5+2)=$

(3) $(6-2)\times 7=\square\times 7$
$=$

(4) $(6+2)\times 7=$

(5) $12\times(8-3)=$

(6) $12\times(8+3)=$

(7) $(18-9)\div 3=$

(8) $(18+9)\div 3=$

(9) $72\div(9-3)=$

(10) $72\div(9+3)=$

(11) $(16\div 4)\times 8=$

(12) $12\times(42\div 6)=$

(13) $(12\times 9)\div 4=$

(14) $96\div(2\times 8)=$

> **Don't forget!**
>
> Calculate the part of the expression in parentheses first.
>
> **Example**
> (1) $5-(3-1)=5-2=3$
> (2) $36\div(2\times 6)=36\div 12=3$

2 Calculate.

4 points per question

(1) $26\times(13+2)=$

(2) $(510-102)\div 17=$

(3) $120\times(120\div 24)=$

(4) $900\div(3\times 5)=$

3 Calculate the multiplication and division first, and then solve the problem.

2 points per question

(1) $23+16\times 2 = 23+\boxed{}$
$=$

(2) $72-13\times 4 =$

(3) $36+48\div 4 = 36+\boxed{}$
$=$

(4) $62-56\div 2 =$

(5) $143+37\times 5 =$

(6) $420-24\times 12 =$

(7) $256+224\div 16 =$

(8) $136-168\div 14 =$

Don't forget!

Unless there are parentheses, calculate the multiplication and division first. Then calculate the addition and subtraction.

Example (1) $5+3\times 4 = 5+12$
$ = 17$

(2) $20-15\div 3 = 20-5$
$ = 15$

---

4 Calculate.

4 points per question

(1) $(18+14)\times 3 =$

(2) $18+14\times 3 =$

(3) $(90-15)\times 5 =$

(4) $90-15\times 5 =$

(5) $(27+36)\div 3 =$

(6) $27+36\div 3 =$

(7) $(84-63)\div 7 =$

(8) $84-63\div 7 =$

(9) $72\div(3\times 4) =$

(10) $72\div 3\times 4 =$

Have you mastered your mixed calculations?

Mixed Calculations

42

1 **Calculate.**

3 points per question

(1) $12 \times 3 + 4 \times 5 =$

(2) $21 \times 4 - 6 \times 3 =$

(3) $36 \div 3 + 48 \div 6 =$

(4) $68 \div 4 - 72 \div 8 =$

2 **Calculate. Then write the appropriate problem numbers in the boxes below.**

2 points per question

① $4 \times 5 + 4 \times 2 =$

② $4 \times 5 - 4 \times 2 =$

③ $7 \times 3 + 2 \times 3 =$

④ $7 \times 3 - 2 \times 3 =$

⑤ $12 \div 2 + 14 \div 2 =$

⑥ $24 \div 3 - 15 \div 3 =$

⑦ $4 \times (5 + 2) =$

⑧ $4 \times (5 - 2) =$

⑨ $(7 + 2) \times 3 =$

⑩ $(7 - 2) \times 3 =$

⑪ $(12 + 14) \div 2 =$

⑫ $(24 - 15) \div 3 =$

(1) ① has the same answer as ☐ .

(2) ② has the same answer as ☐ .

(3) ③ has the same answer as ☐ .

(4) ④ has the same answer as ☐ .

(5) ⑤ has the same answer as ☐ .

(6) ⑥ has the same answer as ☐ .

3 **Write the appropriate number in each box.**

3 points per question

(1) $8 \times 14 + 8 \times 7 = \boxed{} \times (14 + 7)$

(2) $24 \times \boxed{} - 13 \times \boxed{} = (24 - 13) \times 9$

(3) $96 \div 6 + 78 \div 6 = (96 + 78) \div \boxed{}$

(4) $(112 - 52) \div 4 = 112 \div \boxed{} - 52 \div \boxed{}$

4 **Calculate.**

4 points per question

(1) $16 \times 11 + 16 \times 19$
   =

(2) $34 \times 25 - 34 \times 17$
   =

(3) $156 \div 12 + 84 \div 12$
   =

(4) $504 \div 14 - 224 \div 14$
   =

(5) $43 \times 17 - 23 \times 17$
   =

(6) $174 \times 21 - 24 \times 21$
   =

(7) $221 \div 17 + 289 \div 17$
   =

(8) $14 \times 177 + 14 \times 223$
   =

(9) $414 \div 23 - 184 \div 23$
   =

(10) $342 \times 26 + 158 \times 26$
   =

Are you ready to review what you've learned?

Date / /

Name

Level ★★★

Score /100

1 Divide.

3 points per question

(1)
3)52

(2)
8)94

(3)
5)64

(4)
4)83

(5)
7)98

(6)
2)33

(7)
6)75

(8)
9)84

(9)
5)80

(10)
4)56

(11)
4)852

(12)
3)513

(13)
8)601

(14)
5)470

(15)
7)735

(16)
9)670

(17)
6)840

(18)
2)874

(19)
9)853

(20)
7)930

2 Divide.

3 points per question

(1)

$36 \overline{)303}$

(2)

$67 \overline{)536}$

(3)

$45 \overline{)277}$

(4)

$92 \overline{)763}$

(5)

$17 \overline{)96}$

(6)

$24 \overline{)187}$

(7)

$70 \overline{)673}$

(8)

$32 \overline{)774}$

(9)

$45 \overline{)925}$

(10)

$27 \overline{)930}$

3 Calculate.

5 points per question

(1) $740 \div (84 - 47) =$

(2) $108 \div 9 + 35 \times 8 =$

Congratulations! You are ready for **Grade 4 Decimals & Fractions**!

1. Addition & Subtraction Review pp 2, 3

1
(1) 59	(6) 32	(11) 29	(16) 22
(2) 78	(7) 22	(12) 26	(17) 7
(3) 81	(8) 18	(13) 27	(18) 19
(4) 119	(9) 35	(14) 38	(19) 5
(5) 165	(10) 30	(15) 48	(20) 8

2
(1) 158	(6) 118	(11) 252	(16) 143
(2) 175	(7) 218	(12) 265	(17) 568
(3) 389	(8) 522	(13) 544	(18) 556
(4) 583	(9) 348	(14) 260	(19) 162
(5) 823	(10) 262	(15) 249	(20) 192

2. Multiplication & Division Review pp 4, 5

1
(1) 48	(6) 378	(11) 1482	(16) 768
(2) 96	(7) 664	(12) 3017	(17) 1665
(3) 72	(8) 252	(13) 2760	(18) 1431
(4) 180	(9) 954	(14) 6372	(19) 3348
(5) 162	(10) 1692	(15) 276	(20) 4662

2
(1) 9	(11) 6	(21) 8 R 2
(2) 8	(12) 5	(22) 7 R 4
(3) 8	(13) 6	(23) 8 R 2
(4) 7	(14) 6 R 6	(24) 9 R 1
(5) 7	(15) 8	(25) 8 R 2
(6) 7	(16) 7 R 1	(26) 8 R 2
(7) 8	(17) 6 R 2	(27) 9 R 2
(8) 6	(18) 6 R 1	(28) 7 R 2
(9) 8	(19) 6 R 2	(29) 7 R 6
(10) 6	(20) 6 R 4	(30) 9 R 2

3. Mixed Review pp 6, 7

1
(1) 48	(4) 122	(7) 274	(10) 504
(2) 8	(5) 92	(8) 166	
(3) 46	(6) 277	(9) 152	

2
(1) 230	(4) 582	(7) 2322	(10) 1904
(2) 64	(5) 81	(8) 695	(11) 5472
(3) 378	(6) 612	(9) 3360	

3
(1) 1598	(3) 2520	(5) 351	(7) 6633
(2) 3904	(4) 864	(6) 1960	(8) 1300

4
(1) 9 R 2	(6) 2	(11) 6 R 3
(2) 5 R 5	(7) 5 R 2	(12) 8 R 8
(3) 7	(8) 5 R 4	(13) 9 R 2
(4) 7 R 3	(9) 6 R 3	(14) 9 R 6
(5) 8 R 3	(10) 6 R 2	

Advice

If you scored over 85 on this section, review your mistakes and move on to the next section.

If you scored between 75 and 84 on this section, review the last three sections before moving on.

If you scored less than 74 on this section, it might be a good idea to go back to our previous books in order to do an extended review.

If you made many mistakes in **1**, try "Grade 3 Addition & Subtraction."

If you made many mistakes in **2** or **3**, try "Grade 3 Multiplication."

If you made many mistakes in **4**, try "Grade 3 Division."

4. 2-Digits ÷ 1-Digit pp 8, 9

1

(1) $10 \div 2 = \boxed{5}$ $2\overline{)10} = \boxed{5}$

(2) $14 \div 3 = \boxed{4} R \boxed{2}$ $3\overline{)14} = \boxed{4} R \boxed{2}$

2
(1) $2\overline{)12}=6$	(6) $7\overline{)28}=4$	(11) $\boxed{6} R \boxed{2}$	(16) 5 R 6
(2) $3\overline{)18}=6$	(7) $8\overline{)32}=4$	(12) 5 R 1	(17) 8 R 6
(3) $4\overline{)24}=6$	(8) $9\overline{)36}=4$	(13) 6 R 3	(18) 8 R 4
(4) $5\overline{)25}=5$	(9) $2\overline{)15}=\boxed{7} R \boxed{1}$	(14) 6 R 1	
(5) $6\overline{)30}=5$	(10) $\boxed{6} R \boxed{2}$	(15) 6 R 2	

3
(1) $\boxed{13}$	(8) 30	(15) $\boxed{12}$	(22) 18
(2) 14	(9) 32	(16) 13	(23) 19
(3) 20	(10) 40	(17) 20	(24) 24
(4) 21	(11) $\boxed{15}$	(18) 21	(25) 27
(5) 22	(12) 16	(19) 23	(26) 29
(6) 23	(13) 18	(20) $\boxed{14}$	(27) 33
(7) 24	(14) 26	(21) 16	

pp 10, 11

⑤ 2-Digits ÷ 1-Digit

❶
(1) 8 (8) 12 (15) 17 (22) 7
(2) 11 (9) 13 (16) 14 (23) 10
(3) 16 (10) 16 (17) 21 (24) 22
(4) 17 (11) 19 (18) 24 (25) 23
(5) 23 (12) 20 (19) 8
(6) 25 (13) 18 (20) 6
(7) 11 (14) 15 (21) 9

❷
(1) 3 (8) 18 (15) 11 (22) 26
(2) 5 (9) 17 (16) 12 (23) 13
(3) 8 (10) 19 (17) 14 (24) 18
(4) 15 (11) 4 (18) 13 (25) 27
(5) 11 (12) 5 (19) 16
(6) 13 (13) 8 (20) 15
(7) 16 (14) 9 (21) 17

⑥ 2-Digits ÷ 1-Digit
pp 12, 13

❶
(1) 28 (8) 12 (15) 11 (22) 12
(2) 14 (9) 10 (16) 35 (23) 9
(3) 8 (10) 21 (17) 14 (24) 8
(4) 7 (11) 9 (18) 10 (25) 11
(5) 30 (12) 7 (19) 36
(6) 20 (13) 33 (20) 24
(7) 15 (14) 22 (21) 18

❷
(1) 39 (8) 27 (15) 30 (22) 16
(2) 26 (9) 9 (16) 18 (23) 12
(3) 13 (10) 28 (17) 15 (24) 33
(4) 40 (11) 21 (18) 10 (25) 11
(5) 20 (12) 14 (19) 48
(6) 16 (13) 12 (20) 32
(7) 10 (14) 45 (21) 24

⑦ 2-Digits ÷ 1-Digit
pp 14, 15

❶
(1) 6 R 1 (8) 12 R 1 (15) 9 R 2 (22) 11 R 3
(2) 12 R 1 (9) 14 R 2 (16) 11 R 3 (23) 12
(3) 15 R 1 (10) 17 R 2 (17) 13 R 1 (24) 12 R 1
(4) 21 R 1 (11) 18 R 1 (18) 15 (25) 13 R 4
(5) 28 R 1 (12) 20 R 1 (19) 15 R 1
(6) 30 R 1 (13) 21 R 2 (20) 16 R 1
(7) 8 R 2 (14) 8 (21) 10 R 2

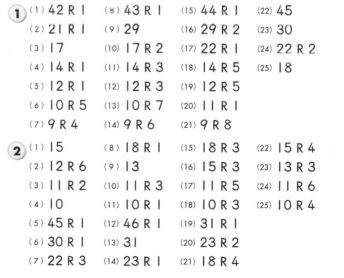

❷
(1) 18 R 1 (8) 20 R 2 (15) 14 R 1 (22) 12 R 3
(2) 20 R 1 (9) 12 R 1 (16) 14 R 3 (23) 10 R 5
(3) 27 R 1 (10) 14 R 3 (17) 14 R 4 (24) 9 R 3
(4) 31 R 1 (11) 15 (18) 12 R 2 (25) 8 R 3
(5) 11 R 1 (12) 16 R 2 (19) 10 R 4
(6) 15 R 2 (13) 13 R 2 (20) 9 R 2
(7) 19 R 1 (14) 13 R 4 (21) 8 R 2

⑧ 2-Digits ÷ 1-Digit
pp 16, 17

❶
(1) 38 (8) 38 R 1 (15) 39 (22) 39 R 1
(2) 19 (9) 25 R 2 (16) 26 (23) 26 R 1
(3) 15 R 1 (10) 15 R 2 (17) 19 R 2 (24) 19 R 3
(4) 12 R 4 (11) 12 R 5 (18) 13 (25) 15 R 4
(5) 10 R 6 (12) 11 (19) 11 R 1
(6) 9 R 4 (13) 9 R 5 (20) 9 R 6
(7) 8 R 4 (14) 8 R 5 (21) 8 R 6

❷
(1) 13 R 1 (8) 16 (15) 16 R 2 (22) 16 R 3
(2) 11 R 2 (9) 11 R 3 (16) 13 R 4 (23) 13 R 5
(3) 9 R 7 (10) 10 (17) 10 R 2 (24) 11 R 6
(4) 8 R 7 (11) 8 R 8 (18) 9 R 1 (25) 9 R 2
(5) 40 (12) 41 (19) 41 R 1
(6) 26 R 2 (13) 27 R 1 (20) 27 R 2
(7) 20 (14) 20 R 2 (21) 20 R 3

⑨ 2-Digits ÷ 1-Digit
pp 18, 19

❶
(1) 42 R 1 (8) 43 R 1 (15) 44 R 1 (22) 45
(2) 21 R 1 (9) 29 (16) 29 R 2 (23) 30
(3) 17 (10) 17 R 2 (17) 22 R 1 (24) 22 R 2
(4) 14 R 1 (11) 14 R 3 (18) 14 R 5 (25) 18
(5) 12 R 1 (12) 12 R 3 (19) 12 R 5
(6) 10 R 5 (13) 10 R 7 (20) 11 R 1
(7) 9 R 4 (14) 9 R 6 (21) 9 R 8

❷
(1) 15 (8) 18 R 1 (15) 18 R 3 (22) 15 R 4
(2) 12 R 6 (9) 13 (16) 15 R 3 (23) 13 R 3
(3) 11 R 2 (10) 11 R 3 (17) 11 R 5 (24) 11 R 6
(4) 10 (11) 10 R 1 (18) 10 R 3 (25) 10 R 4
(5) 45 R 1 (12) 46 R 1 (19) 31 R 1
(6) 30 R 1 (13) 31 (20) 23 R 2
(7) 22 R 3 (14) 23 R 1 (21) 18 R 4

⑩ 3-Digits ÷ 1-Digit — pp 20, 21

1
(1) 1 2 3	(6) 123	(11) 114	(16) 115
(2) 1 2 0	(7) 213	(12) 115	(17) 219
(3) 312	(8) 320	(13) 116	(18) 225
(4) 423	(9) 112	(14) 229	(19) 114
(5) 420	(10) 210	(15) 318	(20) 118

2
(1) 6 0	(6) 15	(11) 26	(16) 39
(2) 40	(7) 14	(12) 20	(17) 28
(3) 30	(8) 64	(13) 18	(18) 24
(4) 24	(9) 42	(14) 16	(19) 21
(5) 20	(10) 32	(15) 52	(20) 19

⑪ 3-Digits ÷ 1-Digit — pp 22, 23

1
(1) 112	(6) 29	(11) 42	(16) 58
(2) 57	(7) 116	(12) 218	(17) 52
(3) 39	(8) 69	(13) 115	(18) 256
(4) 34	(9) 52	(14) 77	(19) 171
(5) 32	(10) 46	(15) 66	(20) 131

2
(1) 88	(6) 126	(11) 1 0 6	(16) 203
(2) 76	(7) 90	(12) 2 0 6	(17) 103
(3) 68	(8) 70	(13) 208	(18) 103
(4) 315	(9) 100	(14) 103	(19) 103
(5) 165	(10) 102	(15) 309	(20) 102

⑫ 3-Digits ÷ 1-Digit — pp 24, 25

1
(1) 306	(6) 84	(11) 90	(16) 90
(2) 189	(7) 272	(12) 70	(17) 81
(3) 102	(8) 164	(13) 107	(18) 409
(4) 108	(9) 117	(14) 106	(19) 301
(5) 94	(10) 103	(15) 98	(20) 189

2
(1) 142	(6) 144	(11) 105	(16) 76
(2) 109	(7) 106	(12) 55	(17) 40
(3) 105	(8) 104	(13) 52	(18) 105
(4) 208	(9) 146	(14) 26	(19) 106
(5) 107	(10) 159	(15) 98	(20) 107

⑬ 3-Digits ÷ 1-Digit — pp 26, 27

1
(1) 308	(6) 75	(11) 77	(16) 89
(2) 159	(7) 226	(12) 348	(17) 80
(3) 107	(8) 136	(13) 174	(18) 360
(4) 92	(9) 114	(14) 117	(19) 240
(5) 84	(10) 86	(15) 102	(20) 144

2
(1) 120	(6) 188	(11) 197	(16) 268
(2) 104	(7) 152	(12) 158	(17) 203
(3) 82	(8) 96	(13) 132	(18) 116
(4) 374	(9) 86	(14) 100	(19) 102
(5) 250	(10) 262	(15) 89	(20) 91

⑭ 3-Digits ÷ 1-Digit — pp 28, 29

1
(1) 410	(6) 423	(11) 96	(16) 97
(2) 206	(7) 282	(12) 288	(17) 437
(3) 138	(8) 170	(13) 145	(18) 292
(4) 119	(9) 142	(14) 125	(19) 219
(5) 105	(10) 122	(15) 109	(20) 176

2
(1) 4 3 5 R 1	(6) 55 R 3	(11) 66 R 5	(16) 172 R 1
(2) 228 R 1	(7) 47 R 4	(12) 57 R 2	(17) 103 R 2
(3) 152 R 2	(8) 41 R 5	(13) 50 R 1	(18) 86 R 1
(4) 158 R 2	(9) 133 R 2	(14) 44 R 5	(19) 73 R 6
(5) 66 R 3	(10) 100 R 1	(15) 258 R 1	(20) 57 R 4

⑮ 3-Digits ÷ 1-Digit — pp 30, 31

1
(1) 288	(6) 64	(11) 66 R 7	(16) 97 R 1
(2) 144	(7) 200 R 1	(12) 388 R 1	(17) 86 R 3
(3) 96	(8) 120 R 1	(13) 194 R 1	(18) 400 R 1
(4) 82 R 2	(9) 85 R 6	(14) 129 R 3	(19) 267
(5) 72	(10) 75 R 1	(15) 111	(20) 160 R 1

2
(1) 114 R 3	(6) 121 R 6	(11) 145 R 1	(16) 105 R 2
(2) 100 R 1	(7) 106 R 5	(12) 102 R 1	(17) 103 R 4
(3) 89	(8) 94 R 7	(13) 58 R 4	(18) 42 R 4
(4) 284 R 1	(9) 220 R 1	(14) 40 R 7	(19) 104 R 4
(5) 170 R 3	(10) 209 R 1	(15) 106 R 2	(20) 28 R 8

⑯ 4-Digits ÷ 1-Digit — pp 32, 33

1
(1) 6 2 3	(5) 228	(9) 519
(2) 241	(6) 843	(10) 2 0 8 0
(3) 200	(7) 427	(11) 1019
(4) 239	(8) 908	(12) 518

2
(1) 2 5 1 5	(6) 1005	(11) 3002
(2) 1259	(7) 889	(12) 2267
(3) 839	(8) 4006	(13) 1067
(4) 2344	(9) 1334	
(5) 1407	(10) 1143	

17　4-Digits ÷ 1-Digit pp 34, 35

1
(1) 653	(5) 514 R 4	(9) 625
(2) 768	(6) 582 R 1	(10) 408 R 7
(3) [6][7][1] R [2]	(7) 1454 R 1	(11) 1034 R 1
(4) 545 R 1	(8) 1022 R 1	(12) 1038 R 3

2
(1) 359	(6) 468	(11) 855 R 4
(2) 203	(7) 947	(12) 864 R 2
(3) 910	(8) 1533	(13) 1308 R 2
(4) 682	(9) 2026	
(5) 468	(10) 866 R 7	

18　3-Digits ÷ 2-Digits pp 36, 37

1

(1)
```
     2 R[3]
21)45
   42
   [3]
```
(5)
```
    [3]R[2]
21)6 5
   [6][3]
     [2]
```
(9)
```
    [3]R[15]
21)7 8
   [6][3]
   [15]
```

(2)
```
     2 R[5]
21)47
   [4][2]
     [5]
```
(6)
```
    3 R 6
21)69
   63
    6
```
(10)
```
    4 R 1
21)85
   84
    1
```

(3)
```
    [2]R6
21)48
   [4][2]
     [6]
```
(7)
```
    3 R[7]
21)70
   [6][3]
     [7]
```

(4)
```
    2 R 7
21)49
   42
    7
```
(8)
```
    3 R 9
21)72
   63
    9
```

2

(1)
```
    [4]R[2]
21)8 6
   [8][4]
     [2]
```
(5) 4 R 15 　　(9) 6 R 3

(2) 4 R 3
(6)
```
    [5]R[2]
21)107
   [1][0][5]
       [2]
```
(10) 5 R 14

(3) 4 R 5
(4) 4 R 10

(7) 5 R 4
(8) 6 R 1

19　3-Digits ÷ 2-Digits pp 38, 39

1
(1) 4 R 4	(5) 3 R 19	(9) 4 R 18
(2) 4	(6) 4 R 11	(10) 5 R 5
(3) 3 R 20	(7) 5 R 3	
(4) 4 R 6	(8) 5	

2
(1) 6 R 4	(5) 6 R 19	(9) 9
(2) 6 R 9	(6) 8	(10) 9 R 15
(3) 7 R 1	(7) 7 R 18	
(4) 7	(8) 8 R 10	

20　3-Digits ÷ 2-Digits pp 40, 41

1
(1) 2 R 3	(5) 3 R 2	(9) 4 R 6
(2) 2 R 13	(6) 3 R 17	(10) 4 R 16
(3) 3 R 6	(7) 4 R 1	
(4) 2 R 28	(8) 3 R 27	

2
(1) 4 R 21	(5) 6 R 4	(9) 8 R 2
(2) 5	(6) 6 R 29	(10) 9 R 21
(3) 4 R 26	(7) 7 R 3	
(4) 5 R 30	(8) 7 R 28	

21　3-Digits ÷ 2-Digits pp 42, 43

1
(1) 2 R 3	(5) 2 R 39	(9) 5
(2) 1 R 40	(6) 4 R 1	(10) 5 R 30
(3) 3 R 2	(7) 3 R 40	
(4) 3	(8) 5 R 3	

2
(1) 6 R 2	(5) 7 R 3	(9) 9 R 1
(2) 6	(6) 7 R 33	(10) 9 R 31
(3) 5 R 39	(7) 8 R 2	
(4) 6 R 34	(8) 8 R 32	

22　3-Digits ÷ 2-Digits pp 44, 45

1
(1) 3	(5) 5	(9) 7
(2) 3 R 9	(6) 5 R 15	(10) 7 R 11
(3) 4	(7) 6	(11) 8 R 9
(4) 4 R 12	(8) 6 R 13	(12) 9 R 2

2
(1) 2	(6) 7 R 9	(11) 6 R 8
(2) 3 R 1	(7) 8 R 16	(12) 7 R 26
(3) 4 R 3	(8) 2 R 6	(13) 9 R 12
(4) 5 R 5	(9) 3 R 14	
(5) 6 R 7	(10) 5	

23 3-Digits ÷ 2-Digits
pp 46, 47

1
(1) 3
(2) 4 R 3
(3) 5
(4) 6 R 17
(5) 7 R 24
(6) 9 R 3
(7) 2 R 36
(8) 3 R 24
(9) 4 R 12
(10) 5
(11) 7 R 6
(12) 9 R 22

2
(1) 2 R 14
(2) 3 R 21
(3) 5
(4) 6 R 22
(5) 7 R 39
(6) 9 R 13
(7) 3 R 8
(8) 4
(9) 4 R 14
(10) 5
(11) 6 R 6
(12) 7 R 17
(13) 9 R 4

24 3-Digits ÷ 2-Digits
pp 48, 49

1
(1) 2 R 22
(2) 3 R 28
(3) 5
(4) 6 R 6
(5) 7 R 17
(6) 9 R 4
(7) 4 R 10
(8) 5
(9) 7
(10) 8 R 10
(11) 9
(12) 9 R 15

2
(1) 4 R 2
(2) 5
(3) 6
(4) 7 R 1
(5) 8
(6) 9 R 7
(7) 2 R 28
(8) 4
(9) 4 R 16
(10) 5
(11) 5 R 35
(12) 7
(13) 9 R 16

25 3-Digits ÷ 2-Digits
pp 50, 51

1
(1) 3 R 4
(2) 4 R 2
(3) 5
(4) 6 R 8
(5) 7
(6) 8 R 4
(7) 3
(8) 4 R 4
(9) 5
(10) 6 R 16
(11) 8
(12) 9 R 4

2
(1) 4
(2) 5 R 5
(3) 6
(4) 6 R 40
(5) 8
(6) 9 R 15
(7) 3 R 9
(8) 4 R 12
(9) 5
(10) 6
(11) 7 R 1
(12) 8
(13) 9 R 7

26 3-Digits ÷ 2-Digits
pp 52, 53

1
(1) 2 R 2
(2) 2 R 42
(3) 4 R 4
(4) 6 R 20
(5) 8
(6) 9 R 5
(7) 2 R 4
(8) 3 R 11
(9) 4 R 8
(10) 5 R 40
(11) 7 R 32
(12) 9 R 24

2
(1) 1 R 54
(2) 3 R 22
(3) 5
(4) 6 R 8
(5) 7 R 51
(6) 9 R 37
(7) 2 R 10
(8) 3 R 5
(9) 4
(10) 4 R 36
(11) 5 R 30
(12) 7 R 18
(13) 9 R 6

27 3-Digits ÷ 2-Digits
pp 54, 55

1
(1) 3 R 3
(2) 3
(3) 4 R 57
(4) 4 R 53
(5) 7
(6) 6 R 57
(7) 3 R 3
(8) 3
(9) 4 R 67
(10) 4 R 63
(11) 7
(12) 6 R 67

2
(1) 3 R 9
(2) 3 R 6
(3) 5 R 5
(4) 5
(5) 9 R 9
(6) 9
(7) 3 R 3
(8) 3
(9) 5 R 5
(10) 5
(11) 6 R 86
(12) 6 R 80
(13) 9

28 3-Digits ÷ 2-Digits
pp 56, 57

1
(1) 2 R 2
(2) 3
(3) 5
(4) 6 R 6
(5) 7 R 35
(6) 9
(7) 4
(8) 6
(9) 6 R 44
(10) 6 R 69
(11) 8
(12) 8 R 67

2
(1) 3
(2) 4 R 4
(3) 5
(4) 6 R 6
(5) 4 R 81
(6) 8
(7) 8 R 77
(8) 4 R 4
(9) 5
(10) 7 R 35
(11) 4 R 91
(12) 7 R 28
(13) 9

29 3-Digits ÷ 2-Digits
pp 58, 59

1
(1) 3 R 3
(2) 4
(3) 4 R 4
(4) 4 R 24
(5) 5 R 9
(6) 5 R 23
(7) 6 R 6
(8) 7
(9) 7 R 17
(10) 8 R 20
(11) 9 R 1
(12) 9 R 10

2
(1) 2 R 3
(2) 3
(3) 4 R 37
(4) 6 R 2
(5) 7
(6) 8 R 34
(7) 9 R 17
(8) 2 R 2
(9) 3
(10) 3 R 45
(11) 5 R 18
(12) 7 R 41
(13) 9 R 24

30 3-Digits ÷ 2-Digits
pp 60, 61

1
(1) 2 R 2
(2) 3
(3) 3 R 55
(4) 6 R 6
(5) 7 R 51
(6) 9 R 19
(7) 2 R 12
(8) 3 R 8
(9) 5 R 7
(10) 5 R 65
(11) 7 R 17
(12) 9 R 35

2
(1) 3 R 3
(2) 4 R 6
(3) 6 R 40
(4) 7 R 77
(5) 9 R 9
(6) 3 R 3
(7) 5 R 17
(8) 6 R 11
(9) 6 R 86
(10) 9 R 39
(11) 2 R 92
(12) 4 R 74
(13) 9 R 59

(31) 3-Digits ÷ 2-Digits

1
(1) 3 R 3 　　(5) 9 R 28 　　(9) 8
(2) 3 　　　　(6) 9 R 19 　　(10) 7 R 8
(3) 7 R 5 　　(7) 7 　　　　(11) 8
(4) 6 　　　　(8) 6 R 7 　　(12) 7 R 11

2
(1) 5 R 14 　　(6) 4 R 54 　　(11) 7
(2) 9 R 19 　　(7) 6 R 17 　　(12) 9 R 6
(3) 4 R 4 　　(8) 6 R 57 　　(13) 6 R 89
(4) 6 R 8 　　(9) 8
(5) 8 R 25 　　(10) 8 R 60

(32) Checking the Answer
pp 64,65

1
(1) $31 \div 4 = \boxed{7} R \boxed{3}$
(2) $31 = 4 \times \boxed{7} + \boxed{3}$
(3) $46 \div 7 = \boxed{6} R \boxed{4}$
(4) $46 = 7 \times \boxed{6} + \boxed{4}$
(5) $68 \div 12 = \boxed{5} R \boxed{8}$
(6) $68 = 12 \times \boxed{5} + \boxed{8}$

2
(1)
```
        6 R 23
  28) 1 9 1
      1 6 8
        2 3
```
$191 \div 28 = \boxed{6} R \boxed{23}$
$191 = 28 \times \boxed{6} + \boxed{23}$

⟨Recalculate⟩
```
        2 8
      ×   6
      1 6 8
      ↓ ↓ ↓
      1 6 8
    +   2 3
      1 9 1
```

(2)
```
        5 R 12
  43) 2 2 7
      2 1 5
        1 2
```
$227 \div 43 = \boxed{5} R \boxed{12}$
$227 = 43 \times \boxed{5} + \boxed{12}$

⟨Recalculate⟩
```
        4 3
      ×   5
      2 1 5
      ↓ ↓ ↓
      2 1 5
    +   1 2
      2 2 7
```

3
(1)
```
        7 R 15
  53) 3 8 6
      3 7 1
        1 5
```
$386 = 53 \times \boxed{7} + \boxed{15}$

⟨Recalculate⟩
```
        5 3
      ×   7
      3 7 1
      3 7 1
    +   1 5
      3 8 6
```

(2)
```
        6 R 44
  64) 4 2 8
      3 8 4
        4 4
```
$428 = 64 \times \boxed{6} + \boxed{44}$

⟨Recalculate⟩
```
        6 4
      ×   6
      3 8 4
      3 8 4
    +   4 4
      4 2 8
```

(3)
```
        6 R 74
  76) 5 3 0
      4 5 6
        7 4
```
$530 = 76 \times 6 + 74$

⟨Recalculate⟩
```
        7 6
      ×   6
      4 5 6
      4 5 6
    +   7 4
      5 3 0
```

(4)
```
        7 R 77
  89) 7 0 0
      6 2 3
        7 7
```
$700 = 89 \times 7 + 77$

⟨Recalculate⟩
```
        8 9
      ×   7
      6 2 3

      6 2 3
    +   7 7
      7 0 0
```

(5)
```
        7 R 89
  99) 7 8 2
      6 9 3
        8 9
```
$782 = 99 \times 7 + 89$

⟨Recalculate⟩
```
        9 9
      ×   7
      6 9 3

      6 9 3
    +   8 9
      7 8 2
```

(33) 3-Digits ÷ 2-Digits
pp 66,67

1
(1)
```
      1 3 R 4
  21) 2 7 7
      2 1
        6 1
        6 3
          4
```
(4)
```
      2 3 R 3
  21) 4 8 6
      4 2
        6 6
        6 3
          3
```
(7)
```
      3 1 R 4
  31) 9 6 5
      9 3
        3 5
        3 1
          4
```

(2)
```
      4 2 R 5
  21) 8 8 7
      8 4
        4 7
        4 2
          5
```
(5)
```
      3 2 R 11
  21) 6 8 3
      6 3
        5 3
        4 2
        1 1
```
(8)
```
      2 1 R 3
  31) 6 5 4
      6 2
        3 4
        3 1
          3
```

(3)
```
      4 5 R 2
  21) 9 4 7
      8 4
      1 0 7
      1 0 5
          2
```
(6)
```
      4 5 R 20
  21) 9 6 5
      8 4
      1 2 5
      1 0 5
        2 0
```
(9)
```
      1 4 R 2
  31) 4 3 6
      3 1
      1 2 6
      1 2 4
          2
```

2
(1)
```
      2 1 R 4
  41) 8 6 5
      8 2
        4 5
        4 1
          4
```
(5)
```
      3 0 R 5
  21) 6 3 5
      6 3
          5
```
(9)
```
      3 0 R 15
  31) 9 4 5
      9 3
        1 5
```

(2)
```
      2 2 R 6
  41) 9 0 8
      8 2
        8 8
        8 2
          6
```
(6)
```
      3 0 R 15
  21) 6 4 5
      6 3
        1 5
```
(10)
```
      3 0 R 30
  31) 9 6 0
      9 3
        3 0
```

(3)
```
      1 2 R 4
  41) 4 9 6
      4 1
        8 6
        8 2
          4
```
(7)
```
      4 0 R 3
  21) 8 4 3
      8 4
          3
```
(11)
```
      2 0 R 3
  31) 6 2 3
      6 2
          3
```

(4) 23 R 14 　　(8) 40 R 14

　93

㉞ 3-Digits ÷ 2-Digits

1
(1) 1̲3̲R1̲2̲ (5) 10 R 21 (9) 31 R 13
(2) 22 R 4 (6) 11 R 13 (10) 18 R 24
(3) 30 R 13 (7) 20 R 14 (11) 29 R 17
(4) 40 R 12 (8) 33 R 2 (12) 21 R 1

2
(1) 20 R 22 (5) 22 R 6 (9) 14 R 47
(2) 25 R 24 (6) 21 R 8 (10) 14 R 19
(3) 20 R 20 (7) 20 R 14
(4) 22 R 35 (8) 15 R 22

㉟ 3-Digits ÷ 2-Digits
pp 70, 71

1
(1) 30 R 15 (5) 28 R 17 (9) 35 R 10
(2) 24 R 10 (6) 23 R 3 (10) 27 R 1
(3) 20 R 7 (7) 19 R 18 (11) 21 R 42
(4) 13 R 3 (8) 12 R 38 (12) 14

2
(1) 31 R 19 (5) 30 R 26 (9) 21 R 29
(2) 20 R 10 (6) 19 R 1 (10) 14 R 40
(3) 42 R 3 (7) 35 R 9
(4) 15 R 12 (8) 23 R 12

㊱ 4-Digits ÷ 2-Digits
pp 72, 73

1
(1)
```
     6̲4̲R1̲
21)1345
   1̲2̲6̲
     8̲5̲
     8̲4̲
      1̲
```
(4)
```
     52 R 5
21)1097
   105
    47
    42
     5
```
(7)
```
     41 R 14
31)1285
   124
    45
    31
    14
```

(2)
```
     6̲9̲R7̲
21)1456
   126
   196
   189
     7
```
(5)
```
     61 R 19
21)1300
   126
    40
    21
    19
```
(8)
```
     54 R 4
31)1678
   155
   128
   124
     4
```

(3)
```
     7̲4̲R1̲3̲
21)1567
   147
    97
    84
    13
```
(6)
```
     94 R 16
21)1990
   189
   100
    84
    16
```
(9)
```
     83 R 27
31)2600
   248
   120
    93
    27
```

2
(1)
```
     32 R 33
41)1345
   123
   115
    82
    33
```
(5)
```
     4̲0̲R5̲
31)1245
   1̲2̲4̲
     5̲
```
(9)
```
     4̲0̲R4̲
25)1004
   100
     4
```

(2) 51 R 32 (6) 40 R 15 (10) 40 R 5
(3) 72 R 35 (7) 50 R 25 (11) 50 R 4
(4) 97 R 23 (8) 60 R 20

㊲ 4-Digits ÷ 2-Digits
pp 74, 75

1
(1)
```
       41
35)1435
   140
    35
    35
     0
```
(5)
```
     55 R 35
42)2345
   210
   245
   210
    35
```
(9)
```
     67 R 39
51)3456
   306
   396
   357
    39
```

(2)
```
     38 R 29
37)1435
   111
   325
   296
    29
```
(6)
```
     53 R 13
44)2345
   220
   145
   132
    13
```
(10)
```
     65 R 11
53)3456
   318
   276
   265
    11
```

(3)
```
     36 R 31
39)1435
   117
   265
   234
    31
```
(7)
```
     48 R 41
48)2345
   192
   425
   384
    41
```
(11)
```
     60 R 36
57)3456
   342
    36
```

(4) 35 (8) 46 R 45 (12) 53 R 11

2
(1) 72 R 40 (5) 60 R 17 (9) 89 R 51
(2) 71 R 24 (6) 57 R 20 (10) 71 R 29
(3) 68 R 56 (7) 92 R 25
(4) 66 R 40 (8) 78 R 3

㊳ 4-Digits ÷ 2-Digits
pp 76, 77

1
(1)
```
     2̲3̲2̲R4̲
21)4876
   4̲2̲
    67
    63
     4̲6̲
     4̲2̲
      4̲
```
(4)
```
     287 R 5
31)8902
   62
   270
   248
   222
   217
     5
```

(2)
```
     323 R 6
21)6789
   63
   48
   42
   69
   63
    6
```
(5)
```
     219 R 10
31)6799
   62
   59
   31
   289
   279
    10
```

(3)
```
     2̲7̲0̲R8̲
21)5678
   4̲2̲
   1̲4̲7̲
   1̲4̲7̲
     8̲
```
(6)
```
     2̲0̲0̲R2̲1̲
32)6421
   6̲4̲
     2̲1̲
```

② (1) 215 R 10   (5) 200 R 12
(2) 125   (6) 195 R 27
(3) 165 R 24   (7) 207 R 1
(4) 161 R 27   (8) 202 R 14

㊴ Division of Large Numbers   pp 78, 79

① (1)
```
        4 R 9
123)5 0 1
    4 9 2
        9
```
(4)
```
        3 R 146
273)965
    819
    146
```
(2)
```
        6 R 13
164)997
    984
     13
```
(5)
```
        3 R 39
306)957
    918
     39
```
(3)
```
        4
237)948
    948
      0
```
(6)
```
        2 R 135
342)819
    684
    135
```

② (1)
```
        4 2 R 30
213)8 9 7 6
    8 5 2
      4 5 6
      4 2 6
        3 0
```
(5)
```
        34 R 34
263)8976
    789
   1086
   1052
     34
```
(2)
```
        40 R 56
223)8976
    892
     56
```
(6)
```
        32 R 240
273)8976
    819
    786
    546
    240
```
(3)
```
        36 R 228
243)8976
    729
   1686
   1458
    228
```
(7)
```
        31 R 203
283)8976
    849
    486
    283
    203
```
(4)
```
        35 R 121
253)8976
    759
   1386
   1265
    121
```
(8)
```
        30 R 186
293)8976
    879
    186
```

㊵ Division of Large Numbers   pp 80, 81

① (1) 13 R 23   (4) 12 R 58
(2)
```
        61 R 26
71)4357
   426
    97
    71
    26
```
(5)
```
        58 R 65
74)4357
   370
   657
   592
    65
```
(3)
```
        13 R 603
713)9872
    713
   2742
   2139
    603
```
(6)
```
        12 R 135
746)9087
    746
   1627
   1492
    135
```

② (1) 11 R 44   (5) 10 R 46
(2) 53 R 11   (6) 48 R 37
(3)
```
        12 R 3
824)9891
    824
   1651
   1648
      3
```
(7)
```
        10 R 871
902)9891
    902
    871
```
(4)
```
        118 R 191
835)98721
    835
   1522
    835
   6871
   6680
    191
```
(8)
```
        108 R 117
913)98721
    913
   7421
   7304
    117
```

㊶ Mixed Calculations   pp 82, 83

① (1) 9−(5−2)=9−[3]
       =6

(2) 2
(3) (6−2)×7=[4]×7
       =28
(4) 56
(5) 60
(6) 132
(7) 3
(8) 9
(9) 12
(10) 6
(11) 32
(12) 84
(13) 27
(14) 6

② (1) 26×(13+2)
   =26×15
   =390
(2) (510−102)÷17
   =408÷17
   =24
(3) 120×(120÷24)
   =120×5
   =600
(4) 900÷(3×5)
   =900÷15
   =60

3
(1) $23+16\times2=23+\boxed{32}$
   $=55$
(2) 20
(3) $36+48\div4=36+\boxed{12}$
   $=48$
(4) 34

(5) 328
(6) 132
(7) 270
(8) 124

4
(1) $(18+14)\times3$
   $=32\times3$
   $=96$
(2) $18+14\times3$
   $=18+42$
   $=60$
(3) $(90-15)\times5$
   $=75\times5$
   $=375$
(4) $90-15\times5$
   $=90-75$
   $=15$
(5) $(27+36)\div3$
   $=63\div3$
   $=21$
(6) $27+36\div3$
   $=27+12$
   $=39$

(7) $(84-63)\div7$
   $=21\div7$
   $=3$
(8) $84-63\div7$
   $=84-9$
   $=75$
(9) $72\div(3\times4)$
   $=72\div12$
   $=6$
(10) $72\div3\times4$
   $=24\times4$
   $=96$

42 Mixed Calculations
pp 84, 85

1
(1) 56
(2) 66
(3) 20
(4) 8

2
① 28
② 12
③ 27
④ 15
⑤ 13
⑥ 3

⑦ 28
⑧ 12
⑨ 27
⑩ 15
⑪ 13
⑫ 3

(1) ⑦
(2) ⑧
(3) ⑨
(4) ⑩
(5) ⑪
(6) ⑫

3
(1) $\boxed{8}$
(2) $\boxed{9}$, $\boxed{9}$
(3) $\boxed{6}$
(4) $\boxed{4}$, $\boxed{4}$

4
(1) 480
(2) 272
(3) 20
(4) 20
(5) 340

(6) 3150
(7) 30
(8) 5600
(9) 10
(10) 13000

43 Review
pp 86, 87

1
(1) 17 R 1
(2) 11 R 6
(3) 12 R 4
(4) 20 R 3
(5) 14
(6) 16 R 1
(7) 12 R 3

(8) 9 R 3
(9) 16
(10) 14
(11) 213
(12) 171
(13) 75 R 1
(14) 94

(15) 105
(16) 74 R 4
(17) 140
(18) 437
(19) 94 R 7
(20) 132 R 6

2
(1) 8 R 15
(2) 8
(3) 6 R 7
(4) 8 R 27

(5) 5 R 11
(6) 7 R 19
(7) 9 R 43
(8) 24 R 6

(9) 20 R 25
(10) 34 R 12

3
(1) 20
(2) 292

Advice

If you made many mistakes in ①, start reviewing on page 8.

If you made many mistakes in ②, start reviewing on page 36.

If you made a mistake in ③, start reviewing on page 82.